# MATT CHRISTOPHER®

## At the Plate with...

# MATT CHRISTOPHER®

At the Plate with...

**Text by Glenn Stout**

LITTLE, BROWN AND COMPANY

New York ❧ Boston

Little, Brown and Company
Time Warner Book Group
1271 Avenue of the Americas, New York, NY 10020
Visit our Web site at www.lb-kids.com

www.mattchristopher.com

First Edition

Matt Christopher® is a registered trademark of Catherine M. Christopher.

Cover photograph by Charles Krupa © Associated Press, AP

Library of Congress Cataloging-in-Publication Data

Stout, Glenn, 1958–
     At the plate with — Ichiro / text by Glenn Stout. — 1st ed.
          p. cm.
     Summary: A biography of the Seattle Mariners hitting and fielding
star who won the MVP and Rookie of the Year Award in 2001 and became the first successful Japanese player in the Major Leagues.
          ISBN: 978-0-316-13679-2          ISBN: 0316136794
     1. Suzuki, Ichiro, 1973 — Juvenile literature.   2. Baseball
players — Japan  — Biography — Juvenile literature.   [1. Suzuki,
Ichiro, 1973–   2. Baseball players.   3. Japan — Biography.]
I. Christopher, Matt.   II. Title.

GV865.S895 S76 2003                                        2002033259

10 9 8 7 6 5 4 3 2

COM-MO

Printed in the United States of America

# Contents

# MATT CHRISTOPHER®

## At the Plate with...

# Chapter One

## The American Pastime in Japan

Ichiro had it all. Almost.

In his native Japan, outfielder Ichiro Suzuki (ee-cheer-oh soo-ZOO-kee) of the Orix Blue Wave was the most famous celebrity in the entire country. Since becoming a professional ballplayer and signing with Orix of the Pacific League in 1993, he had become the most popular and exciting athlete in Japan. Beginning in 1994, Ichiro won the league batting title for seven consecutive seasons. He won three MVP awards and was named to the league all-star team every season from 1994 to 2000.

Most observers considered Ichiro the best all-around player in the history of Japanese baseball — a great hitter and a fast runner who could steal bases with ease and chase down fly balls in right field. His throwing arm was the strongest and most accurate

1

in the game. The Orix team knew his worth — Ichiro was the highest-paid baseball player in Japan.

By the year 2000, his fame in Japan had transcended sports. A poll determined that Ichiro was the most recognizable person in Japan, more familiar than the emperor or the prime minister or the biggest television star. Although "Ichiro" is a common name in Japan, meaning "first son," fans referred to Ichiro Suzuki by his first name only, just as American golfer Tiger Woods is known primarily as "Tiger."

Japanese fans of all ages had fallen in love with Ichiro. Wherever he went he was mobbed by fans who treated him as if he were a pop star or a famous actor, and he was hounded for autographs. At his home ballpark, fans could buy all sorts of merchandise with his name or picture on it — teacups, keychains, T-shirts, towels, caps, stickers, even cell phones. Young women thought he was handsome and collected photographs of him. People copied his style of hair and clothing. On one occasion he was spotted wearing a pair of yellow sneakers. During the next few months, Japan was swept with a crime wave as gangs of youths robbed people who were wearing the same type of sneakers.

2

Newspaper and magazine writers reported on almost every aspect of Ichiro's life. He could hardly leave his home without being followed by photographers and television crews. He was constantly being offered parts in movies and in television programs. He dated famous Japanese actresses and models. Books about him became instant bestsellers.

Yet despite all his fame and notoriety, Ichiro was unfulfilled. He felt that he had accomplished as much as he could playing baseball in Japan, and he was tired of living in the spotlight. As one Japanese observer noted, "Even when he went to the restroom, people would follow him. It was not happy for him." Ichiro wanted a new challenge and a new start where no one knew who he was.

He also wanted to prove that he was more than just the best baseball player in Japan. He wanted to be considered one of the best ballplayers in the world. To do that, he knew he would have to play in the United States — in the major leagues.

In the United States, Ichiro was virtually unknown. Even experienced major league players and scouts knew little about him. While some had heard that he was Japan's best player, no one was certain if he were talented enough to play in the major leagues, much less become a star. Some even questioned whether or not he could make a major league team. After all, no Japanese player had ever succeeded in the major leagues.

But Ichiro was confident that he would succeed. In the fall of 2000, he announced his plan to play in the United States. "I want to be the first player to show what Japanese batters can do in the major leagues," he said. In one short year, he would demonstrate that he was, indeed, one of the best players in the world.

Only a few years earlier, the notion that a Japanese ballplayer could be one of the best in the game would have been laughed at. Although baseball has a long and storied history in Japan, few people either in Japan or in the United States have believed that Japanese baseball measures up to its American counterpart.

Baseball was first brought to Japan in the 1870s, when American teachers of English in Japan taught the game to their students. Japanese society places great value on the concept of teamwork, and base-

4

ball provided a shining example of it. The Japanese people adopted the game, and its popularity grew quickly. By the turn of the century, baseball was being played all over the country, particularly in high schools and colleges. American teams such as the 1913 Chicago White Sox occasionally toured Japan. These teams were often surprised by the passion that Japanese fans had for baseball, and they were impressed by the rapidly improving skills of Japanese players.

A visit by the great Babe Ruth in 1934 enraptured Japanese fans. Like American fans, the Japanese loved watching the Babe hit home runs. He won the crowd over with his personality, too. Two years later, in 1936, the first professional Japanese baseball league was formed.

Before the league could get under way, the Japanese government embarked on a series of policies that resulted in the December 7, 1941, surprise attack on the American naval base at Pearl Harbor in Hawaii. This attack led to war between the United States and Japan.

As Japan put all its resources into the war effort,

the Japanese professional baseball league had to cut back the number of teams and the length of the season. In 1945, the league was forced to suspend play.

When the war ended with the surrender of Japan in 1945, American troops occupied the country and tried to help Japan rebuild. In their spare time, many American servicemen played baseball. The soldiers and the Japanese people soon realized that the love of baseball was something that both countries had in common. Japanese fans turned out in droves to watch the Americans play, and American military officials encouraged the Japanese to resume playing baseball. Professional baseball soon blossomed again in Japan.

Japan used the American major leagues as its model and created two baseball leagues — the Pacific League and the Central League — that each played a 130-game regular season schedule. At the end of the season, the two league champions then played each other in the Japan Series.

Japanese professional baseball was very successful in the years after the war. To strengthen ties between the nations, squads of American major leaguers would often tour Japan in the off-season to play exhibition games against Japanese all-star teams. By the 1950s, American baseball officials noted the improving skills of the Japanese players and predicted that one day Japanese players would reach the American major leagues. To help speed the development of the game in Japan, Japanese baseball officials began to send a small number of Japanese players to the United States to work out with major league teams in spring training.

In 1964 the San Francisco Giants and the Nankai Hawks of Japan reached an agreement that allowed several Hawks to play in the Giants' minor league system. Pitcher Masanori Murakami became the first Japanese player to play professional baseball in the United States. When Murakami was successful in the minors, the Giants called him up to the major leagues.

Although he became a valuable relief pitcher, Murakami didn't stay with the team long. The Giants and the Hawks disagreed over which team held the rights to Murakami. Murakami became homesick and didn't want to continue playing in the United States. After the 1965 season, he returned to Japan.

At about the same time, American players made

their mark in the Japanese leagues. In 1962 a small number of Americans began playing professionally in Japan. Japanese teams offered American ballplayers high salaries to play in Japan. Japanese baseball was not yet as competitive as the major leagues. Most American players who went to Japan were either aging former stars whose skills were dwindling, or players of average ability who found out they could become stars in Japan.

The Americans quickly discovered that the Japanese had taken the American national pastime and made it their own. While the rules of the game remained the same, the style of play was much different. Japanese teams emphasized fundamentals far more than their Major League Baseball counterparts, and sometimes they held practices that lasted all day! Since Japanese players were smaller in stature and hit fewer home runs than American players, the Japanese tried to scratch out single runs with bunts and hit-and-run plays. Most Japanese pitchers didn't throw as fast as the American ones, so they depended more on curveballs and other off-speed pitches.

The fans behaved differently too. In Japan, they

cheered, chanted, and pounded drums throughout the entire game; some teams even had cheerleaders to keep the crowd excited. American players realized that in order to succeed in Japan, they would have to adapt to the Japanese culture and style of play.

Many of the American players eventually returned to the United States. When they did, they often talked about the best players in Japan, such as slugger Sadaharu Oh, who hit more home runs in his professional career in Japan than Hank Aaron (Aaron holds the major league record of 755).

Year by year the quality of play in Japan continued to improve. Major league teams touring in Japan learned they had to take the contests seriously and play well in order to win. Occasionally, they even lost a game or two to their Japanese rivals. Japanese baseball fans looked forward to the day when their leagues would be on the same level as the American major leagues. Some dreamed of a day when Japanese teams would be a part of the major leagues.

But after Masanori Murakami returned to Japan in 1965, no Japanese players came to the United States to play in the major leagues for nearly thirty years. They were prevented from doing so by their contracts in Japan and by their traditional Japanese values, which placed a great deal of value on loyalty. Even when players were legally allowed to change teams, they rarely did, because Japanese fans expected players to remain loyal to their original teams. To do otherwise would be considered selfish, a trait that is almost foreign to Japanese society.

But under increasing influence from Western countries, Japanese society was slowly changing. Younger people didn't always accept traditional Japanese values. By the 1990s, Japanese baseball players began to demand the same rights as players in American baseball. They wanted to be able to change teams and secure the best possible contracts.

Finally, in 1994, star Japanese pitcher Hideo Nomo decided to leave Japan for the United States. He hired an agent who examined his contract and discovered that if Nomo announced his retirement, he would be released from his Japanese contract. He quickly "unretired" in the United States and signed a lucrative contract with the Los Angeles Dodgers.

Nomo was a sensation with the Dodgers and immediately became one of the best pitchers in the major leagues. His unique pitching motion earned him the nickname "the Tornado," and American batters found his pitches difficult to hit.

Nomo's success sent shock waves through the Japanese baseball organization. Officials feared that other star players would follow the same path as Nomo, and that Japanese baseball would suffer. Similarly, American baseball officials wanted to keep Japanese baseball intact to ensure that the talent pool of Japanese players remain strong. So officials from both countries reached an agreement in December of 1998 that would control the number of Japanese players who could play in the United States. After nine years as a professional, all Japanese players would become free agents, eligible to sign a contract anywhere in the world. But if a player wanted to play in the United States *before* he became a free agent, then the U.S. team that signed that player would have to pay the Japanese team for the right to acquire him.

During the next few seasons, a handful of Japanese players signed the American teams. Some, like pitcher Hideki Irabu, who joined the Yankees in 1998, struggled. Others, like Seattle Mariner relief pitcher Kazuhiro Sasaki, were more successful. But no position player — meaning no players other than pitchers — made the jump from Japan to the United States. Most observers believed that major league pitching was too fast for Japanese hitters, and that the Japanese style of play wouldn't work in the United States.

However, as baseball fans all over America would soon learn, there were few players anywhere in the world with the skills of Ichiro.

## Chapter Two:
### 1973–1994

### Introducing Ichiro

Ichiro Suzuki was born on October 22, 1973, in the Aichi Prefecture of Japan. A prefecture is similar to a state or province. Ichiro grew up in Toyoyama, a suburb of the large city of Nagoya, about 150 miles from the Japanese capital of Tokyo.

Ichiro's father was a big baseball fan. He worked long hours in a factory every day and liked to relax by watching baseball. He had played when he was younger but hadn't been good enough to play professionally. When his son Ichiro was born, he looked forward to teaching him how to play.

Ichiro began learning the game when he was only three years old. Whenever his father had the chance, he would take his son to a local park for practice. They would play catch, throwing the ball back and forth to get loose, and then Ichiro's father would pitch so that Ichiro could practice batting. As Ichiro's skills improved, his father began hitting ground balls and pop-ups to him so he could practice his defense.

At first, Ichiro loved just being with his father. But he soon discovered that he loved baseball too. When his father wasn't available for practice, Ichiro played with other children in his neighborhood.

When Ichiro joined his first organized team at age eight, he already knew the basics of the game. His father coached the team. Although they played games only on Sunday, nearly every other day Ichiro practiced with his father. He was soon one of the best players his age in Toyoyama.

By the time he reached high school, Ichiro was one of the best players in the Aichi Prefecture. Although he stood just 5 feet 9 inches and barely weighed 150 pounds, his arm was powerful. He was the star pitcher for his team, Aiko-Dai Meiden. His fastball was timed at more than ninety miles per hour. He began to dream of playing professional baseball.

At the end of each high school baseball season, more then 4,000 Japanese high school teams participate in a ten-day tournament known as the *Koshien*. Held in Koshien Stadium near Osaka, the tournament is one of the highlights of the year for Japanese baseball fans and is as popular in Japan as the World Series is in the United States. In his final year of high school in 1991, Ichiro led his team into the Koshien tournament.

Although Aiko-Dai Meiden didn't win the tournament, Ichiro played well. On the mound, he dominated the opposition with his fastball. He also hit well and played stellar defense in the outfield. Japanese professional baseball scouts took notice. After the tournament, Ichiro hoped he would be drafted by a professional team.

Because he pitched the ball so fast, most teams thought of him primarily as a pitcher. But even by Japanese baseball standards, Ichiro was considered small. Pro teams were concerned about his size and were afraid he might not be physically strong enough for the demands of pitching. Despite his great fastball, selecting him early in the draft would be a risk. If he had been bigger, he would have been a top pick, but most observers expected him to be picked in the fifth or sixth round.

Ichiro was worried. Although he enjoyed pitching, he enjoyed hitting and playing in the outfield even more. He knew that if he became a pro pitcher he would get to play once or twice a week, and that his arm might not hold up. But if he became an out-fielder, he would get to play every day.

One Japanese team, the Orix Blue Wave, who play in Kobe, Japan, wasn't interested in Ichiro as a pitcher. They liked the way he hit the ball, ran the bases, and fielded. He was extremely fast and ath-letic, and the Blue Wave scouts thought those talents would go to waste on the pitcher's mound. In No-vember of 1991, the Blue Wave selected Ichiro in the fourth round of the draft. Ichiro was thrilled when he learned that they wanted him as a hitter and an outfielder.

Ichiro quickly signed a contract and began to pre-pare for spring training. The Blue Wave decided that Ichiro needed more experience, so in 1992, when Ichiro was nineteen, the officials sent him to play for their minor league team.

Ichiro got off to a quick start and played well, hit-ting over .300. In mid-season Ichiro was brought up to play for the Blue Wave.

He was excited and nervous about stepping onto the same field with so many of the baseball stars he had watched on television. Although he played sparingly, getting only 95 at-bats in 40 games, he hit a respectable .253 and didn't make an error in the outfield. Ichiro hoped he would make the Blue Wave for good in 1993.

But in the spring, the Blue Wave again decided he needed more experience and sent him back to the minors. The move seemed to help Ichiro flourish. After 48 games he was hitting a robust .371 with 8 home runs. The Blue Wave brought him up to the majors again.

Blue Wave manager Shozo Doi had very firm ideas about how the game of baseball should be played. Despite Ichiro's record of success in the minors, Doi didn't like the way Ichiro stood at the plate and swung his bat at the ball. As the pitcher prepared to throw, Ichiro, who bats left-handed, would hold his bat straight out in front of him with his right hand. Then he would twirl it around and slowly pull it back over his left shoulder, shuffling his feet as the pitcher wound up. Then, as the pitch approached, he would swing the bat like a pendulum from his upper body, parallel with the ground, taking a big swing for a small player.

Doi didn't approve of Ichiro's style. He told him bluntly, "You'll never hit that way." He demanded that Ichiro change his approach. He wanted Ichiro to stand still in the batter's box and take a short, choppy swing.

But Ichiro didn't feel comfortable that way. He resisted Doi's efforts to change his style. In Japan, it is considered bad manners not to follow instructions. Doi thought that Ichiro was disrespectful and buried him on the end of the bench. On the rare occasions when he played, it was usually as a pinch runner or defensive replacement.

Ichiro was miserable. He lost his confidence. When he did manage to get an at-bat, he tried too hard and usually got out. He played even less than the year before and hit only .188 for the season. He began to wonder if he would ever get a chance to prove that he could play.

Fortunately for Ichiro, he wasn't the only member of the Blue Wave to struggle under manager Doi. The team played poorly in 1993, and in the off-season Doi was replaced by Akira Ogi. Ichiro hoped for a fresh start under the new manager.

At spring training in 1994, Ogi didn't try to change

18

the way Ichiro hit. In fact, he liked the way Ichiro swung the bat. Even though he had a big swing, Ichiro didn't try to pull the ball all the time but simply hit it where it was pitched. Even if a pitch fooled him, he rarely swung and missed. With his bat speed, any ball within reach was a potential hit. Ichiro began to relax and soon started hitting again.

But as the season began, the manager did have one suggestion. The Japanese are very superstitious about names. The way a name sounds and the way it looks when written are believed to bring either good or bad luck. Manager Ogi told Ichiro that he should change his name to change his luck. He would be a new player in 1994, and he needed a new name. Ogi told Ichiro to drop his last name, Suzuki, and use only the name "Ichiro."

At first, Ichiro wasn't certain he liked the idea. Both his first name and last name were very common in Japan, like the name "John Smith" in the United States. He was afraid that if he began calling himself just "Ichiro," people would think he was getting a big head. No player in Japan had ever used just his first name before. But Ogi insisted that the change would help him.

Despite Ichiro's misgivings, as soon as he changed his name he became hot at the plate, spraying hits all over the ballpark. He needn't have worried about the fans, either. They quickly responded to the new name. Although there were many other players with the first name "Ichiro," and many others who shared the common last name "Suzuki," there was only one player known simply as "Ichiro." With the way he was playing, everyone soon learned who he was.

Early in the season Ichiro's batting average hovered around .400. While some expected him to fade as the season wore on, Ichiro just kept hitting the ball.

Day after day he reached a base with a hit. On the rare occasion that he was hitless, he still got on base with a walk. Sportswriters soon started keeping track of the number of consecutive games in which Ichiro got on base.

Ichiro's streak reached an incredible 69 games before he was finally kept off base on August 26, a record for Japanese baseball. By then, every baseball fan in Japan knew who Ichiro was. In only a few short months he went from being nearly unknown to becoming the most popular ballplayer in Japan. Every time he stepped to the plate, fans chanted

"Ichiro! Ichiro!" over and over, and they waved signs that read: ICHIRO IS ICHIBAN, which in Japanese means, "Ichiro is number one."

As the end of the 1994 season approached, fans started keeping track of another record that Ichiro was approaching. In Japan, the record for hits in one regular 130-game season was 191. Two hundred hits in one season was considered unreachable.

But Ichiro was on fire. In September, he closed in on the record and broke it in the 116th game of the season. Six games later, he exploded with four hits in one game to reach the 200-hit barrier. With another record out of the way, fans now turned their attention to Ichiro's batting average. He was hitting just under .400. No one in Japanese baseball had ever hit .400 before. The record was .389. Eight games remained in the season.

Just as it seemed Ichiro would set the record, he went into his only slump of the season, failing to get a hit in back-to-back games for the first time all year. He finished the season with a .385 average, still 62 points higher than his closest rival that season. In 130 games, Ichiro went hitless in only 13 games.

Despite being only twenty years old, Ichiro had

become a full-fledged star. He was named the MVP of the Pacific League and observers began to compare him to other Japanese baseball stars. Some of Japan's greatest former players analyzed his hitting style and deemed it sound. A professor at a university studied Ichiro's swing and announced that he had more bat speed than the great slugger, Sadaharu Oh. Clearly, Ichiro had the potential to become one of the best hitters in the history of Japanese baseball. Some believed that he already was the best.

People started comparing Ichiro to the best players in the United States and wondered how well Ichiro would play in the major leagues. A respected broadcaster and former pitcher, Suguru Egawa, said that Ichiro would have trouble catching up to the speed of American pitching.

Up to that point, Ichiro had listened to others discuss his ability without comment. But now he spoke out.

"As long as a ball is thrown by a human being, I have the confidence to hit any pitch, no matter how fast it comes," he said publicly. Then Ichiro made sure that no one in Japan would think he was bragging or being disloyal — traits the Japanese frown on. In typical Japanese fashion he added, "But I've never thought of playing in the major leagues."

He paused for a moment, as if considering the idea for the first time, and said, "If I did, I'd probably hit only .250." During the next few seasons, Ichiro's opinion of his own ability would change, and he would begin to dream about playing in the major leagues.

# Chapter Three:
## 1995–2000

## Japan's Best Player

Over the next several seasons, Ichiro got better, hitting with more power, driving in more runs, and stealing more bases. In 1995 and 1996, he not only repeated as batting champion and MVP but he also led his team, the Blue Wave, to the Japan Series — the Japanese equivalent of the World Series. Although the Blue Wave failed to win the championship, Ichiro played well.

After Japanese pitcher Hideo Nomo signed with the Los Angeles Dodgers in 1995, more and more people asked Ichiro if he wanted to play in the major leagues. He was secretly thinking about it, but he didn't like to talk about it. He was still under contract with the Blue Wave and years away from free agency.

But Ichiro kept improving every year, winning the batting title each season and adding to his reputation. After the 1996 season, he received his first opportunity to measure his skills against American players.

Ichiro was named to the Japanese all-star squad, which was scheduled to host a series of games against a similar team of American players. In his first game, batting against pitchers Pat Hentgen and Pedro Martinez, Ichiro went 2-for-3 with 2 walks. Japan surprised the Americans with a 6–5 win.

Ichiro was the best player on the Japanese team. But after playing once more, he didn't play again until the eighth and final game of the series so that other Japanese players could have an opportunity to play.

Despite having sat out for nearly a week, Ichiro bounced back in the series finale, batting 3-for-5 against Hentgen and Martinez. The game ended in an 8–8 tie. The Americans won the series by winning four games and losing twice with two ties. In the three games in which Ichiro played, each team won once with one tie. Ichiro's performance gave him more confidence. Even though it would be several more seasons before he would be granted free agency, he began to seriously consider the possibility of playing in the United States.

Most American sportswriters who covered the series were surprised by Ichiro's performance and thought it was just luck. But New York Mets manager Bobby Valentine, who had managed in Japan in 1995, was not surprised at all. After having watched Ichiro for a full season, Valentine was telling people that Ichiro was "one of the five best players in the world." Few believed him.

Although the Blue Wave failed to contend for the pennant the next two seasons, Ichiro continued to dominate Japanese baseball, winning batting titles in both 1997 and 1998. After the 1998 season, he received a second opportunity to test his skills against the Americans in another post-season series between all-stars of both countries.

Once again, he was the most impressive Japanese player on the field. In one game he went 3-for-5 with 2 stolen bases, and he led the Japanese team to their first win of the series. In another, he knocked in the only run in a 1–0 Japanese victory.

Cleveland Indians manager Mike Hargrove, who managed the American team, told the Japanese press that, "Before I got here, I hadn't heard of Ichiro, but I am very impressed. He has above-average ability in hitting and throwing."

The American squad beat the Japanese team in the series, but the Americans were forced to play their best in order to win. Some of the American players, perhaps embarrassed by the fact that the series was so close, tried to downplay the abilities of Japanese players. "Fastballs are tough for them," said American pitcher Curt Schilling about Japanese hitters. Schilling and Al Leiter, another pitcher, dismissed Ichiro, questioning his ability.

The Blue Wave realized that Ichiro was itching to play in the United States. To keep him happy in the off-season, they worked out a special arrangement with the Seattle Mariners, who were partially owned by the Japanese company Nintendo. Ichiro and several teammates were allowed to work out with the Mariners in spring training and would be eligible to play in the first four games of the exhibition season. The Blue Wave also signed Ichiro to the most lucrative contract in the history of Japanese baseball, worth $4.15 million American dollars. Blue Wave officials hoped that Ichiro would appreciate their gesture and remain loyal to the team.

Ichiro was thrilled to practice with the Mariners at their training camp in Peoria, Arizona. He followed major league baseball closely in the newspapers and on the Internet. His favorite American player was Seattle outfielder Ken Griffey Jr.

Ichiro worked hard to fit in with the Mariners, and his temporary teammates were impressed. "We talk every day," said Mariner pitcher Jamie Moyer in reference to his conversations with Ichiro through an interpreter. "His biggest question is always, 'Can I play in the U.S.?'"

Based on watching him for only a few weeks, Moyer wasn't certain if Ichiro would hit as well as he did in Japan, but he was struck by Ichiro's running speed and by his throwing arm. "I think he's faster than anyone over here [in the major leagues]," he said. He also thought Ichiro's arm was as strong as anyone's in the majors.

The Mariners' front office was even more impressed. Batting coach Jesse Barfield, who'd played in Japan himself, said, "If anybody in Japan could come over and have success, it's Ichiro, because he's so fundamentally sound in everything he does." Roger Jongewaard, the team's vice president of scouting, said, "He could be a leadoff hitter or a number two hitter and get a couple of hundred hits for us. He'd be perfect in our lineup."

But Jongewaard was careful to make it clear that the Mariners weren't trying to steal Ichiro, and that they respected the existing agreement between American and Japanese baseball organizations. They understood that Ichiro wouldn't be eligible for free agency until 2001. When he was asked if the Mariners would be interested in acquiring Ichiro, Jongewaard would only say, "It might be something we could work on down the road."

Ichiro also spoke carefully when he was asked if he wanted to play for the Mariners. "I want to face the best in baseball," he said.

Unfortunately, just as the exhibition season got under way, Ichiro became ill and couldn't play much. He returned to Japan for the 1999 season and had another spectacular year, hitting .343 even though his season was cut short when he was hit by a pitch that broke his wrist. But now that Ichiro had had a taste of American baseball, he began to speak more openly of his desire to play in the majors. He told his Blue Wave teammate, American pitcher Willie Banks, that "the major leagues is my type of baseball." According to Banks, Ichiro said, "Everybody in the States is so relaxed and everyone in Japan is so uptight." He liked the fact that American practices lasted only two or three hours, leaving time to relax and do other things.

He was also increasingly bothered by all the attention he received in Japan. When he had trained with the Mariners, he was treated as if he were just another player. He could even go out to dinner and go shopping without being pursued by fans. That was impossible for him in Japan. He had become so popular that when he decided to marry his girl-friend, Yumiko, a Japanese television personality, they traveled to Los Angeles so they could have a private ceremony.

At the beginning of the 2000 season, many Japanese baseball fans wondered if it would be the last season for Ichiro in Japanese baseball. The Blue Wave could force him to remain with them through the 2001 season, but the team would get nothing if Ichiro signed with a major league team once he became a free agent. If, however, the Blue Wave allowed Ichiro to sign with an American team before his contract was up, the major league team would have to pay the Blue Wave several million dollars.

In his mind, Ichiro had already decided to leave. But he was determined to have his best year as a Japanese player. In mid-season, he was hitting above .400, and with only a month left in the season he was hitting .387. Baseball fans all over Japan looked forward to Ichiro's final games to see if he could average .400.

Unfortunately, it was not to be. He pulled a muscle in his side and doctors told him it would take a month to heal. The Blue Wave was out of the pennant race, and it appeared as if Ichiro's season, as well as his career in Japan, was over. Except for hitting .400, there was little left for Ichiro to accomplish in Japan. Now he could finally set his sights on the United States and the American major leagues. For the first time since 1994, he would be just another player.

# Chapter Four:
## 2000–2001

### Ichiro the Mariner

As the off-season approached, Blue Wave Team President Yutaka Okazoe reluctantly agreed to allow Ichiro to play in the United States. According to the agreement between the two countries, American teams were allowed to submit bids to the Blue Wave. Once the team accepted a bid, the American team would have a month to work out a contract with Ichiro. If Ichiro couldn't work out an agreement, he would have to return to Japan for another season.

Ichiro made the announcement on October 12, 2000. "For a number of years I have had the feeling that I would like to take a shot at playing in the majors," he told reporters. "I'm happy I've reached an agreement with the club to open up this possibility."

"We really don't want to let him go," said Okazoe,

but added he wanted to allow Ichiro to "pursue the dream that will make him happy."

Ichiro thanked the Japanese fans and said, "I hope they will be happy for me."

The next day, in the Blue Wave's final game of the season, he made a last appearance in uniform to say good-bye. His side was still too sore for him to hit, but in the ninth inning he came into the game to play right field and received a long, heartfelt ovation from Orix fans. Then he walked off the field and into his future.

The Blue Wave officially made Ichiro available to Major League Baseball teams on November 1, 2000, and then sat back and awaited offers. They expected to receive millions of dollars.

Most observers expected the Mariners to be one of the teams to bid on Ichiro. In recent years they'd traded away such big stars as pitcher Randy Johnson and outfielder Ken Griffey Jr. Although they made the playoffs in 2000, they were eliminated by the Yankees and were now facing the possibility of losing star shortstop Alex Rodriguez, who was now a free agent. It seemed as if Seattle needed new talent.

But no one was quite sure which teams other than Seattle would be interested in Ichiro. Understandably, Ichiro was nervous, telling the press, "I feel like a high school player a couple of days before the draft: very nervous, very excited, very eager."

Many major league teams were uncertain about Ichiro's skills. They wanted players who could hit home runs, and they questioned whether Ichiro, despite having displayed some power in Japan, could reach the fences in the bigger American ballparks. They considered him a singles hitter, and as one baseball insider commented, "We've all got plenty of those."

The Blue Wave hoped that interest in Ichiro would spark a bidding war as teams tried to outbid each other. But the war never broke out. The New York Yankees, baseball's wealthiest club, passed on Ichiro. They'd been disappointed in the performance of Hideki Irabu and didn't want to take a chance on another player from Japan.

Only a few teams, including the New York Mets, decided to bid on Ichiro. Mets manager Bobby Valentine was sure Ichiro was a star and wanted him badly, but the Mets' front office wasn't as enthusiastic. No other team valued Ichiro as much as the Mariners, who were more familiar with Ichiro and more confident of his ability to succeed in the major leagues than any other team.

In 2000, the team had moved from the home-run-friendly Kingdome to Safeco Field, a big, new, state-of-the-art ballpark that favored a team built around speed and defense. The Mariners thought Ichiro would be perfect for the new style of play that the Mariners would have to use to win at Safeco. On November 10 the Blue Wave announced that the Mariners had bid more than $13 million for the rights to negotiate a contract with Ichiro.

Ichiro was ecstatic. He had always hoped to play for a team on the West Coast of the United States because many inhabitants of the large cities on the West Coast have a Japanese heritage, and Ichiro would fit in. The Seattle Mariners had always been his favorite major league team, and in 2000 the Mariners had signed the star Japanese relief pitcher Kazuhiro Sasaki. Ichiro was friends with Sasaki and knew that having another Japanese player on the team would make it easier for him to adjust to life in America. "Being able to play for Seattle is the realization of a dream," Ichiro said.

A few days later, Ichiro's agent and the Mariners reached an agreement on a three-year contract that, with incentives, could be worth as much as $18 million. In the previous few weeks Seattle baseball fans had heard a lot about Ichiro. Now they could hardly wait to get their first look at him.

The Mariners introduced Ichiro at a big press conference at Safeco Field in Seattle on November 30, 2000. Local newspeople were shocked when nearly fifty members of the Japanese media flew over for the press conference. They had been told that he was popular in Japan, but they had no idea of just how famous Ichiro was in his native land.

The American press quickly learned how much Japan loved Ichiro when a group of Japanese schoolgirls who were visiting Seattle on a class trip arrived at Safeco Field for a tour just as Ichiro arrived. As soon as they saw him they started squealing with delight and chasing after him.

Speaking with the help of an interpreter (at that

time Ichiro knew only a few words of English), Ichiro confidently laughed and joked through the press conference, telling the media that he probably wouldn't hit many home runs because he had "skinny arms." He told them that signing his contract with the Mariners "was the best day of my life."

Ichiro asked the Mariners to help him find a three-bedroom apartment. They did, but they were curious why Ichiro, who had no children, needed the extra room. "To take my practice swings," he told them. He spent the next few months living quietly in Seattle with his wife, Yumiko, working out at the ballpark in the morning, and learning his way around the city.

He loved the fact that he could live like a normal person. The large number of Japanese-Americans in the Seattle area made it possible for Ichiro to blend in. "I really enjoy being able to go anywhere without people noticing me," he commented at the time. Yumiko, he said, "is even happier than I am." For the first time in their marriage she felt as if she had Ichiro to herself. Apart from the Japanese press, everyone else was leaving him alone.

"Of course, I have some pressure here," he told a

reporter, "but compared to the pressures I have had in the past, this pressure is nothing. When I play in Japan everyone expects me to be the leading hitter every year.

"I will never regret the fact I came over here and tried to play in America," he said. "I have had a dream to come over here and because of that I have never regretted what I did. I am making my dream come true."

But Ichiro knew that to really fulfill his dream, he would have to prove on the field that he was one of the best players in the world, and that he could help make his team better. He looked forward to the start of spring training.

Ichiro's new teammates were equally eager for him to start. In the off-season, Alex Rodriguez had left the team as a free agent and signed with the Texas Rangers. The Mariners would be a different team without Rodriguez's powerful bat. They hoped that Ichiro would help them adjust to his absence.

During the next few months, the Mariners would learn a lot about their new player and the new team he would help create.

# Chapter Five:
## 2001

## Spring Dreams

Ichiro arrived at spring training in Peoria, Arizona, in mid-February. His new teammates greeted him with a combination of curiosity and disbelief. They were anxious to see if he could help the team, but they were stunned by the attention he received. They couldn't believe the number of Japanese reporters who had traveled to Arizona to cover Ichiro. Nearly 150 members of the Japanese press showed up to report on Ichiro's activities at camp. In contrast, only a handful of American reporters covered the Mariners during the spring, and only about a dozen followed the team during the regular season.

The other Mariners quickly learned that Ichiro was eager to make friends. The Mariners had employed a translator to make it easier for Ichiro and his teammate Sasaki to communicate. Ichiro greeted his new

Ichiro smacks a single in a game against the Chicago White Sox in May 2001.

One of the fastest players in the game, Ichiro puts on speed to steal third.

Ichiro fans show their support for the Japanese import.

Top All-Star pick Ichiro warms up during practice on July 9, 2001.

The constant center of media attention, Ichiro patiently gives the press some time before the July 10, 2001, All-Star Game.

Ichiro gives it his all when a fly ball is hit to deep right field.

Ichiro and a teammate exchange high fives after Ichiro crosses home plate to add another run to Seattle's scorecard.

Mariner Mike Cameron gives Ichiro a hug. Thanks to newcomers like Ichiro, the Mariners far exceeded anyone's expectations in the 2001 season.

Ichiro listens with a smile as an interpreter relays the good news that he's been chosen as the American League's Most Valuable Player for 2001.

A rookie no longer, Ichiro heads for first on a double in one of the first games of the 2002 season.

# Ichiro's Year-by-Year Batting Stats

| Year | Club | Avg. | G | At-Bats | Runs | Hits | 2B | 3B | HR | RBI | SB |
|------|------|------|---|---------|------|------|----|----|----|-----|----|
| 2001 | Mariners | .350 | 157 | 692 | 127 | 242 | 34 | 8 | 8 | 69 | 56 |
| 2002 | Mariners | .321 | 157 | 647 | 111 | 208 | 27 | 8 | 8 | 51 | 31 |
| 2003 | Mariners | .312 | 159 | 679 | 111 | 212 | 29 | 8 | 13 | 62 | 34 |
| Career | | .328 | 473 | 2018 | 349 | 662 | 90 | 24 | 29 | 182 | 121 |

# Ichiro's Year-by-Year Fielding Stats

| Year | Club | POS | G | GS | E | DP | FLD % |
|------|------|-----|---|----|---|----|----|
| 2001 | Mariners | RF | 152 | 148 | 1 | 2 | .997 |
| 2002 | Mariners | CF | 3 | 3 | 0 | 0 | 1.000 |
| 2002 | Mariners | RF | 150 | 146 | 3 | 0 | .991 |
| 2003 | Mariners | RF | 159 | 156 | 2 | 4 | .994 |
| Career as CF | | | 3 | 3 | 0 | 0 | 1.000 |
| Career as RF | | | 461 | 450 | 6 | 6 | .994 |

# Ichiro's Career Highlights

**1996:**

Pacific League MVP

Pacific League Batting Champion

Pacific League On-Base Percentage Leader

Pacific League Gold Glove

Member of the Pacific League All-Star Team

# Ichiro's Career Highlights

**1997:**
Pacific League Batting Champion
Pacific League Gold Glove
Member of the Pacific League All-Star Team

**1998:**
Pacific League Batting Champion
Pacific League Gold Glove
Member of the Pacific League All-Star Team

**1999:**
Pacific League Batting Champion
Pacific League On-Base Percentage Leader
Pacific League Gold Glove
Member of the Pacific League All-Star Team

**2000:**
Pacific League Batting Champion
Pacific League On-Base Percentage Leader
Pacific League Gold Glove
Member of the Pacific League All-Star Team

**2001:**
First Japanese-born position player in Major League Baseball
Member of the All-Star Team
American League Rookie for April, May, August, and September
Voted American League Rookie of the Year
Voted American League MVP
American League Batting Title
Gold Glove Award

**2002:**
Member of the All-Star Team
Gold Glove Award

**2003:**
Member of the All-Star Team
Gold Glove Award

teammates warmly and accepted their good-natured ribbing with a big smile. At the same time, he acted as if the media crush didn't bother him, telling American reporters that "this is nothing new to me."

Japanese reporters tried to explain to their American counterparts just how popular Ichiro was in Japan. "He is bigger than Elvis Presley," explained one. "He is bigger in Japan than Michael Jordan is in America," offered another. Every baseball fan in Japan wanted to see if Ichiro could succeed in the major leagues.

Ichiro was already looking forward to the regular season. He told reporters he could hardly wait to see "the parks with the most history," such as Yankee Stadium and Fenway Park. He didn't seem intimidated by the prospect of facing major league pitching and said, "I'm really looking forward most to facing Pedro Martinez. He was with the major league team that came to Japan in 1996, just before he became a superstar. I'm anxious to see how much he has improved. And I'm anxious to see how much I've improved against him."

Ichiro was in great shape, and in workouts he impressed all his teammates with his speed, throwing arm, and ability to catch the ball in the outfield. But everyone was curious to see if he could hit major league pitching.

During the first few weeks of the exhibition season schedule, no one was sure whether Ichiro would thrive at the plate. Batting left-handed, all he seemed able to do was slap at the ball and hit grounders to the left side of the infield. Ichiro beat out some for infield hits, and others rolled into the outfield for singles, but many major league scouts weren't impressed. Ichiro didn't seem to have much batting power. "Pitchers are knocking bats out of his hands," sniffed one scout.

Seattle manager Lou Piniella was a little concerned. Ichiro appeared to be overmatched by pitchers with a good fastball. Piniella had originally hoped that Ichiro would hit .300, but he now privately thought the outfielder would be lucky to hit .270 or .280 — nearly one hundred points below his career batting average in Japan.

When Piniella finally expressed his concern to Ichiro, Ichiro told him not to worry. He told the manager that he was hitting the ball on the ground to the left side on purpose. "I'm just setting them up," he said in reference to the opposing pitchers. He wanted other teams to underestimate his ability so that when the regular season began, he could surprise them. A few days later in an exhibition game, Ichiro decided to show Piniella that he could pull the ball with power. As if he'd flipped a switch, Ichiro pulled the ball easily, hitting hard line drives and even cracking a long home run.

His teammates were impressed. "Nobody is that good," said Seattle outfielder Al Martin. "This isn't Little League. You don't just walk into your first spring training, hang around, and set people up." But the Mariners were beginning to discover that Ichiro *was* that good. He was a special player.

After toying with the notion of placing Ichiro third in the batting order, Piniella decided to have Ichiro lead off. Seattle scouts had timed him running from home to first base in only 3.7 seconds — faster than anyone else in the major leagues. If a ground ball hit by Ichiro weren't fielded cleanly, he would almost certainly beat the throw to first. With Ichiro on base in front of the Mariners' big hitters, such as designated hitter Edgar Martinez, first baseman John Olerud, and second baseman Bret Boone,

Piniella was convinced that Ichiro could use his speed to score a lot of runs.

When the Mariners left camp at the end of March and traveled to Seattle for the start of the regular season, Mariners fans weren't particularly enthusiastic over the team's prospects in the 2001 season. After losing stars like Ken Griffey Jr. and Alex Rodriguez in the past two seasons, the fans weren't expecting much from the club. Hardly anyone in baseball thought the Mariners could win the American League Western Division, in which the Oakland Athletics looked like a powerhouse. Reaching the playoffs, even as a wild card team, seemed like wishful thinking for the Mariners.

But the fans were intrigued by Ichiro and excited to see him play. A maximum-capacity crowd turned out at Safeco Field on opening day as the Mariners took on the Athletics. Many Japanese fans had flown to Seattle for Ichiro's major league debut.

When Ichiro stepped into the batter's box at 7:15 P.M. in the bottom of the first inning and Oakland pitcher Tim Hudson delivered the first pitch, flashbulbs went off in every corner of Safeco Field. Ichiro was a major leaguer at last.

At the same time back in Japan, where it was 11:15 A.M., some twelve million Japanese fans huddled around televisions to watch the game on TV. A Japanese station had made arrangements to televise most Mariners games. The Japanese fans were even more interested in Ichiro than Seattle fans were on opening day. As one Japanese reporter commented, "A lot of Japanese baseball fans took an early lunch today."

But the most interested spectator of all was a Japanese man in the second row behind the Mariners' dugout. Ichiro's father, the man whom Ichiro credited with teaching him how to play baseball, had traveled from Japan to see his son play his first game in the major leagues.

The first pitch to Ichiro was called a ball. On the next pitch, Ichiro smacked a grounder to second base.

He broke out of the box quickly and ran as fast as he could. But Oakland second baseman Jose Ortiz fielded the ball cleanly and threw him out by a step.

As Ichiro trotted back to the dugout, he let out a big sigh of relief. At last he was a major leaguer! And now that he had gone to bat once, he could relax and concentrate on the game.

Ichiro went hitless in his next two at-bats, and the Mariners were trailing the Athletics. Ichiro came up again in the seventh inning, facing pitcher T. J. Mathews.

Mathews pitched carefully, trying to protect Oakland's two-run lead. But Ichiro got a good look at a low fastball and smacked the pitch up the middle.

Mathews reacted and reached for the ball, but he was too late. The ball bounded into center field. Ichiro had collected his first base hit!

He stood on first base as the Seattle crowd gave him a huge ovation, then he called time and asked for the baseball. The Athletics tossed the ball to a Seattle coach for safekeeping. From his seat behind the dugout, Ichiro's father beamed with pride. His son had gotten a hit in the major leagues!

Oakland's scouting report on Ichiro warned that he was a threat to steal at any time, and his base hit shook up the A's pitcher. Worried about Ichiro, Mathews failed to concentrate hard enough on the next few Seattle hitters. Ichiro didn't steal, but Edgar Martinez eventually knocked him home for his first major league run, and the Mariners scored again to tie the game.

Ichiro came to the plate again in the eighth inning after teammate Carlos Guillen reached base on a walk. Ichiro knew that in this situation — a tie game in a late inning — it was up to him to move the runner into scoring position.

Ichiro hadn't bunted for a base hit in eight years. The A's expected him to hit away.

But Ichiro had set them up. Once he noticed that Oakland's infielders were playing deep in hope of turning a double play, he knew what he had to do. Bunt! If he did so successfully, the A's wouldn't have enough time to turn a double play, and Guillen could move into scoring position.

Ichiro was careful not to tip off the A's about his plan. He stood in the batter's box and performed his usual ritual, holding the bat in front of him with his right hand, then drawing it back over his shoulder as he entered his crouch, nervously lifting his feet up and down.

But as relief pitcher Jim Mecir began his windup, Ichiro sprang into action.

He quickly spun his body to face the pitcher, and then stuck his bat out over the plate, parallel to the ground, holding it loosely so the bunt would roll slowly along the ground, forcing the fielder to charge in and rush his throw.

Ichiro made contact, and the ball rolled down the first baseline in what is known as a drag bunt. Ichiro sprinted like a cheetah down the line.

A's first baseman Jason Giambi and Mecir scrambled after the ball, completely surprised. Neither could decide who should field the ball. By the time someone did, Ichiro was already on first base and Guillen had run all the way to third base. Ichiro had collected another hit. But more important, he had helped his team by moving Guillen into scoring position.

A few moments later, John Olerud lofted a fly ball to the outfield. Guillen tagged up on the sacrifice fly and scored easily. The Mariners led, 5–4!

Kazuhiro Sasaki shut down the A's in the top of the ninth and the Mariners sent their fans home happy with a 5–4 win. Ichiro had made the difference in the game. In fact, if it weren't for their two Japanese players, Ichiro and Sasaki, the Mariners probably wouldn't have won.

The crowd at Safeco Field roared as the Mariners ran off the field with their first victory of the season.

As Ichiro reached the infield, he exchanged high fives with his teammates. And all over Japan, Ichiro fans beamed with pride.

When Ichiro left the field and returned to the Mariners' clubhouse, reporters, most of them from Japan, swarmed him. "Of course I am glad to have this day over," he said with a faint smile. "And winning the game is a bonus. Now it's time to come back out tomorrow and start over."

By becoming the first Japanese position player to appear in the major leagues, Ichiro had already fulfilled one dream. Now he was prepared to pursue another.

# Chapter Six:
## 2001

### Incredible April

Ichiro and the Mariners both got off to good starts as Seattle took two of three from Oakland, and Ichiro, after going hitless in his second game, went 2-for-4 in the series finale. The team then flew to Texas to play the Rangers.

The game received a great deal of attention, for it would be the first time that Alex Rodriguez, the Ranger shortshop, would play against his old team. The presence of Ichiro was an afterthought.

But when the game started, Ichiro took over. He sparked a four-run, first-inning rally with a leadoff double as the Mariners jumped into the lead. The Rangers fought back to tie the game and send it into extra innings, and Ichiro again proved to be the difference. In the tenth inning, he pulled the ball hard down the right field line for a game-winning home run, his first in the major leagues! The Mariners won, 9–7. So far in the young season, Ichiro was hitting a whopping .421. Seattle didn't appear to miss Alex Rodriguez at all.

Ichiro impressed everyone with his play. Even when he made an out he usually advanced a base runner. But just ten days into the season, on April 11, Ichiro made a play that had everyone in baseball talking about his abilities.

As the Mariners played the A's again in Oakland, Seattle manager Lou Piniella decided to give Ichiro a rest. He wanted Ichiro to remain strong all season, so he kept Ichiro out of the starting lineup. But in the eighth inning, the game was still scoreless. The Mariners needed Ichiro. Piniella asked Ichiro to pinch-hit.

Despite the fact that he wasn't in the starting lineup, Ichiro had made certain he stayed warm in case he was needed. Periodically during the game he had gone into the clubhouse and loosened up by riding a stationary bike and hitting against a pitching machine under the stands. When he stepped to the plate, he felt relaxed, and he looped a single into left field.

The hit sparked a rally. Ichiro scored the first run of the game to put the Mariners ahead. In the bottom of the inning he played in right field as Seattle pitcher Aaron Sele tried to hold the slim lead.

Oakland outfielder Terrence Long, one of the fastest players in baseball, came to bat. He singled up the middle. Then pinch hitter Ramon Hernandez stepped up to the plate.

Out in right field, Ichiro quickly sized up the situation. When Ichiro is in the field, he thinks ahead. Before every pitch he tries to imagine what he would do if the ball were hit toward him. That way, he isn't surprised by anything that happens.

He reminded himself that if the ball were hit into the gap between outfielders, then he would have to make certain he got to the ball quickly, before it passed him and rolled all the way to the wall. If it did pass him, Long would probably score easily. If the ball were hit into the air, Ichiro would have to catch and quickly throw the ball to second base so that Long couldn't tag up and advance to second. If the ball were hit in front of him, Ichiro would have to charge it and come up throwing to try to prevent the speedy runner from making it to third base. In a close game, he knew the Mariners couldn't afford to let the A's runner get to third, where he could score on a fly ball, a ground-out, or even a wild pitch.

Ichiro also took into consideration the hitter, Ramon Hernandez. Before every series, the Mariners go over a scouting report on the other team. Ichiro didn't know much about many of the players, so he always paid close attention to what his coaches told him about the opposition. He remembered that Hernandez, a right-handed hitter with some power, liked to pull the ball to left field. As Hernandez stepped into the batter's box, Ichiro took a few steps toward left field and a step or two in. If Hernandez hit the ball to right field, he probably wouldn't hit it as far or as hard as if he pulled it to left.

Ichiro then peered in as the Mariner catcher gave Sele the sign for the pitch. Ichiro saw that the catcher wanted the ball thrown to the outside part of the plate. Ichiro knew that if Sele pitched to that spot, Hernandez would probably hit the ball toward Ichiro. Now, Ichiro was ready for anything.

Hernandez wisely didn't try to pull the outside pitch. Instead, he hit the ball just as Ichiro expected, spanking the pitch into right field. The Oakland crowd roared as the ball sailed over the infield and then hit the ground for a base hit. Long took off from first base. From his first step he was determined to advance to third base. As he admitted later, he thought to himself, "It's going to take a perfect throw to get me."

Out in right field, Ichiro was ready. He knew that Long was fast and as soon as the ball was hit he assumed that Long would try to make it all the way to third base. When the ball bounced his way he charged it to make the play as quickly as possible.

He caught the ball on the hop with his glove while running at full speed. Then, in one motion, he wound up and threw to third base, nearly falling to the ground on his follow-through.

The ball left his hand and all that fans saw was a white blur, like a shooting star, streaking only ten or twelve feet off the ground toward third base. Long was already halfway between second and third, in full stride. Mariner third baseman David Bell straddled third base, prepared to take the throw, while shortstop Carlos Guillen stationed himself halfway between Ichiro and Bell, prepared to cut off the throw if Bell yelled that it was off line.

But Bell stayed silent as the ball rocketed his way. All eyes were on third base.

Just as Long began to slide, the ball shot past him. Bell, holding his glove just a few inches off the ground in front of the base to make a tag, didn't even have to move his hands when the ball flew in. The ball struck his glove like a dart piercing a bull's-eye. Bell then dropped his glove to the ground just as Long slid in to the base.

The third base umpire hesitated for a moment to make certain that Bell had held onto the ball. As soon as he saw the ball in Bell's glove, the ump shot his right hand into the air. "Out!" he yelled. The crowd was silent and Long sat on the ground with a look of disbelief on his face.

Ichiro had made a perfect throw!

Up in the press box, reporters sat dumbfounded. They had never seen a better throw. One of them later called it "a 200-foot lightning bolt." Another said that Ichiro's throw "needs to be framed and hung on the wall at the Louvre, next to the *Mona Lisa*. It was that much a thing of beauty." (The Louvre is an art museum in France, and the *Mona Lisa* is a famous painting in the Louvre by Leonardo da Vinci.)

Third baseman David Bell later admitted, "I knew he [Ichiro] had a great arm, but I was surprised." Even the Oakland crowd was impressed. After an awkward moment of silence, the crowd gave Ichiro a nice ovation. Even though the throw had hurt their team, the Oakland fans appreciated such a spectacular play.

The Mariners held on to win, 3–0. Later that night on sports shows all over the country, fans everywhere saw Ichiro's throw again and again as the play, which Seattle fans soon started calling simply: "The Throw," was shown over and over. From that moment, most American baseball fans began to realize that Ichiro was more than just another ballplayer. He was a *great* ballplayer — the kind of player who threatens to make a stellar play every time he steps onto the field.

A few days later, Ichiro made another spectacular play, leaping up and reaching over the fence in Seattle to steal a home run from Rafael Palmeiro of the Texas Rangers.

In the games that followed, both Ichiro and his team played far better than anyone had expected. Sparked by Ichiro's play, the Mariners jumped out to a 15–4 record. Ichiro's batting average hovered over .350, and he was among the league leaders in runs scored.

In a matter of weeks, Ichiro, the player whom few Seattle fans had heard of at the start of the season, had become the most popular player on the team. Few Mariners fans were complaining about having lost Ken Griffey Jr. and Alex Rodriguez anymore. Ichiro was more than making up for their loss.

Now many American fans started acting like their Japanese counterparts. Every time he stepped on the field they started chanting: "I-CHI-RO! I-CHI-RO!" Ichiro merchandise became bestsellers at Safeco Field. The press called it "Ichiro-mania."

And Japanese fans remained intensely interested in watching Ichiro. Broadcasts of Mariners games drew such high ratings in Japan that some people were afraid that the Japanese would lose interest in their own major leagues. Japanese travel companies even began to sell special travel packages so fans could fly from Japan to Seattle to see Ichiro. So many Japanese fans began attending Mariners games that the team had to hire Japanese-speaking vendors to serve them at Safeco Field. There was so much interest in Ichiro in Japan that one Japanese newspaper was offering $2 million for a picture of Ichiro in the locker room!

Near the end of April, the Mariners traveled to New York to play the World Champion New York Yankees. Even though it was early in the season, everyone expected the Yankees to provide a stiff test of the Mariners. Around baseball, there were still some people who doubted that the Mariners could keep up their winning pace and that Ichiro could continue to play so spectacularly. Many thought that the Yankees, with such star pitchers as Roger Clemens, Mike Mussina, and Mariano Rivera, would shut down the Mariners and Ichiro.

Wrong! Led by Ichiro's four hits, tough defense, and a stolen base, the Mariners swept the Yankees in three straight games. The scouts who had once questioned Ichiro's ability were silenced, although some still believed that as the season stretched on, pitchers would figure out how to pitch to Ichiro. But Ichiro was determined not to allow that to happen.

Manager Lou Piniella tried to keep the pressure off his surprising team and its new star, reminding everyone that "it's still early," and that the Mariners still had more than 140 games left to play. But Ichiro's teammates already recognized his contributions to the team.

. Center fielder Mike Cameron told an interviewer that Ichiro was "the engine of our train," the player who'd been carrying the team during the first month of the season. Ichiro's teammates were so impressed by his abilities that they nicknamed him "the Wizard," and believed that he could do anything on the baseball field.

At the end of April, the Mariners had an incredible record of 20–5. Even if they won only half of the remaining games, they would probably make the playoffs. Everyone on the team was playing well, including second baseman Bret Boone, who was hitting better than he ever had hit in his life, and closer . Kazuhiro Sasaki, who was earning saves at a record pace. But most Mariners recognized that Ichiro was the main reason they had started off so strongly.

At the end of the month Ichiro was named "American League Rookie of the Month." Although some complained that because Ichiro had played in the Japanese major leagues he wasn't technically a rookie, his .336 batting average and 17 runs scored proved his value to the team.

Ichiro and the Mariners entered May with optimism. They were determined to show everyone that April hadn't been a fluke.

# Chapter Seven:
## 2001

### A Fast Start

So far during the young season, Ichiro and the Mariners had been able to sneak up on the opposition. But now the secret was out. Ichiro and the Mariners were *great*. For the rest of the season they knew the other teams would try their best to stop them.

But some people still debated over whether Ichiro was really as good as he seemed to be. One ESPN television analyst, former big league manager Buck Showalter, said he believed that Ichiro had "a chance to hit .400," and become the first major leaguer to do so since the great Ted Williams.

However, Showalter's counterpart, former pitcher Rob Dibble, refused to believe that Ichiro could keep it up. He said that he would run naked through Times Square if Ichiro continued to hit well and won the batting title. That was his way of saying Ichiro couldn't possibly continue to hit so well. When Seattle manager Lou Piniella was told about Dibble's comment, he called the broadcaster and later said, "I told him he better start working on his tan."

In mid-May the Mariners traveled to Toronto for a three-game series against the Toronto Blue Jays. Before they arrived, a member of the Blue Jays' front office told the press that the reason Ichiro was hitting so well was because pitchers were pitching him outside, to his strength. The Blue Jays, he announced, had figured this out and planned to "bust" Ichiro inside, trying to jam him and move him off the plate.

Ichiro wasn't bothered by the strategy. In fact, as he had proved during spring training, he thrived on pitchers' false expectations of him. If they pitched him inside, he was confident he could pull the ball and do so with power.

Three days later, the Blue Jays came to the same conclusion. While the Blue Jays kept trying to bust Ichiro inside, he kept pulling the ball with power, collecting nine hits in three days, including two doubles and two triples. The Mariners swept the Blue Jays and Ichiro's batting average approached .400.

In 37 games so far, Ichiro had collected a hit in 35 of them, including a 23-game hitting streak that ended with the last game versus the Blue Jays. "This kid can hit," said manager Piniella. "He just can hit. He knows how to play. He's a player, period. It's pretty seeing him hit those line drives all over the outfield. The ball jumps off his bat. There's no question he's lifted the level of the entire team, that guys feed off his adrenaline and execution."

Slowly but surely Ichiro and the Mariners were convincing more people that they really were as good as they appeared to be. With men on base, Ichiro was hitting better than .500. He had struck out only a handful of times and rarely swung at a pitch and missed it. Some people were already touting him as a candidate for both the Rookie of the Year Award and the Most Valuable Player Award. And others were saying the Mariners were now the odds-on favorites to win the World Series!

Seattle led the Western Division by more than ten games, an incredible spread for so early in the season. For Ichiro, the only thing he didn't like was that he had become so popular that he found it almost as difficult for him to live in Seattle and retain his privacy as he found it in Japan. Already, it was virtually impossible for him to leave his apartment or hotel without being swarmed by both fans and the press.

Japanese reporters were particularly aggressive. They followed him everywhere. Ichiro's spectacular performances had made him more popular than ever in his native country. Fans were obsessed with Ichiro. One Japanese reporter noted that when Ichiro was playing, virtually every television in Japan was tuned in to the Mariners. "When Ichiro comes to bat," the reporter explained, "people in restaurants stop eating and watch."

Ichiro was the talk of baseball, on pace to break the all-time record of 257 hits in one season, set by George Sisler in 1920.

When the Mariners played the Yankees for the second time in mid-May, Ichiro turned out another incredible performance. Although the Mariners lost the first game of the series, 14–10, Ichiro was almost unstoppable. In the second inning of that game he singled, then stole both second and third base, and scored a run. Three innings later he singled again and eventually scored another run. In the seventh he squelched a Yankees rally by making a tremendous running catch. He topped off his performance with a double, driving in a run. As he bent over second base and tried to catch his breath, Derek Jeter, the Yankee star shortstop, walked up to Ichiro and said with a smile, "Take it easy, man. That's enough."

Two days later, he collected another hit that had all the Yankees talking. Yankee ace pitcher Roger Clemens threw Ichiro a split-fingered fastball to the outside corner, a pitch that looks like a straight fastball until the last instant, when it dives to the ground. When thrown correctly, it is virtually impossible for most players to hit.

But Ichiro wasn't like most players. He somehow stayed with the pitch as it dropped, nailing it into left field for a double. Clemens just shook his head in wonder. Teammate Edgar Martinez later told reporters that Ichiro had the best hand-eye coordination in baseball.

After the first 50 games of the season, Seattle's record was an unbelievable 38–12, the tenth-best record after 50 games in the history of Major League Baseball. No player on the team was more responsible for that than Ichiro.

Even on those rare occasions when he didn't hit,

Ichiro still found a way to help the Mariners win. In Baltimore on May 29, he saved the game by making two tremendous catches in the right field corner, the last a shoestring catch he made while running full speed to end the game. "He's amazing to watch," said teammate Mark McLemore later.

But his teammates were just as impressed with Ichiro the person as they were with Ichiro the player. Although communication was difficult, they appreciated the fact that Ichiro tried to speak English and allowed his teammates to teach him funny English phrases. He learned to greet teammates by saying "Whassup?" like a hip-hop star, and if a teammate asked him how he was, he would respond, "I'm chillin' like Bob Dylan," even though he had no idea who Bob Dylan, a famous American folk singer, was.

"Guys constantly give him a hard time," explained Bret Boone, "which is a sign that they like him." Ichiro was not egotistical, and he had a good sense of humor. "He's fun to have around," added his teammate.

He also worked harder than many of his teammates, often taking 200 or more practice swings every day. He would have taken even more, but

Seattle's batting practice pitchers were getting sore arms from pitching to him so much.

To no one's surprise, Ichiro won the Rookie of the Month Award for May as well, and when the first results of balloting for the All-Star Game were released in early June, Ichiro had more votes than all but one other American League player, catcher Ivan Rodriguez of the Texas Rangers. *Sports Illustrated* magazine even put Ichiro's picture on the cover.

The Mariners were the hottest team in baseball, winning fifteen straight games from May 22 to June 8, effectively answering the question of whether or not they would make the playoffs. Their success was due not only to Ichiro but also to the many other Mariners who were playing top ball. In center field, Mike Cameron was playing the outfield just as well as Ken Griffey Jr. had and was hitting much better than expected. Second baseman Bret Boone emerged as one of the most prolific RBI-men in baseball, and DH Edgar Martinez continued to be one of the most productive hitters in the game. The Mariners' pitching staff, led by starters Jamie Moyer, Freddy Garcia, Aaron Sele, and Sasaki, was the deepest in baseball.

As mid-season approached, Ichiro began to reflect on the first half of the season. He was delighted when he learned that not only had he been elected to start in the All-Star Game, which was scheduled to be played in Seattle, but also he had received more votes than any other player. "I thought I had little chance of being selected," he said. "It means a lot to me, because in just a few months Seattle has become my special town."

Over the next few months, Ichiro would make every city in the American League his special town.

# Chapter Eight:
## 2001

### All-Star Ichiro

Ichiro entered the All-Star break with a record most other players envied. Not only was he on a first-place team but he was hitting a solid .345, almost identical to his career average in Japan. He wasn't hitting with quite as much power as he had in Japan, but as a leadoff hitter he wasn't expected to hit home runs. The Mariners just wanted him to get on base, and he was doing that in virtually every game.

American League All-Star Game manager Joe Torre of the Yankees immediately recognized Ichiro's value to his team. When he made out his batting order for the game, he put Ichiro in the leadoff spot, hoping he could do for the American League team what he had been doing for the Mariners all year.

Safeco Field was filled to the brim for the All-Star Game on July 10, and Ichiro was joined on the team by fellow Mariners Edgar Martinez, Bret Boone, Mike Cameron, Jeff Nelson, and Freddy Garcia. Torre put Ichiro in center field because the other two starting outfielders on the American League team, Manny Ramirez and Juan Gonzalez, weren't very good fielders.

Ichiro didn't mind. He was honored to be selected to the team and looked forward to playing. The game was receiving a great deal of attention because it would be the last All-Star Game appearance of Baltimore Oriole Cal Ripken, one of baseball's most popular players. Ripken had decided to retire at the end of the season.

The National League would start pitcher Randy Johnson of the Arizona Diamondbacks. Johnson had once started for the Mariners and worn uniform number 51 — the same number now worn by Ichiro. Standing 6 feet 10 inches, the left-handed pitcher was almost impossible for left-handed batters to hit.

His fastball approached 100 miles per hour and his slider was devastating, dipping away from left-handed batters just as the pitch approached the plate. Many left-handed batters asked for the day off when Johnson was pitching.

But Ichiro was unafraid. As he had said years before, he was confident he could hit a ball thrown by any pitcher.

Baseball fans looked forward to seeing how Ichiro would do against Johnson, as did the other All-Star players. Few observers gave him much of a chance against baseball's greatest strikeout pitcher. Edgar Martinez told one reporter, "The only advice I have for Ichiro is to make sure the pitches he swings at are in the strike zone."

The National League came to bat first and quickly went out without scoring. The NL team took the field and Ichiro approached the batter's box.

The fans in Safeco Field gave him a huge ovation as he stepped in. Then the crowd grew quiet and still as the imposing Johnson toed the rubber and looked hard at Ichiro. Compared to Johnson, Ichiro looked like a little boy.

Johnson wound up and fired a blazing fastball. Ichiro watched it pass by without taking the bat from his shoulder, getting his first look at Johnson's delivery and gauging his speed.

"Strike!" called the umpire.

Ichiro had gotten a good look at the pitch and felt confident. Johnson threw hard, but Ichiro was sure he could hit him.

Johnson wound up and threw again. As the fastball rocketed in, Ichiro kept his eye on the ball and swung hard at the pitch on the inside corner. He hit a hard grounder toward right field, between NL first baseman Todd Helton and the first base line. As soon as he hit the ball, Ichiro started running as fast as he could.

Helton, playing off the line, ranged far to his left toward the line and snagged the rapidly bouncing ball. As he did, Johnson broke from the mound to cover first base.

Ichiro's short legs were pumping fast and furiously. Helton spun and threw the ball toward the base as Johnson prepared to take the throw and step on the bag.

But no player in baseball could run to first base faster than Ichiro. His speed had already helped him collect thirty infield hits for the season.

Johnson took the throw a step off the base and reached with one of his long legs to touch the bag for the out. But Ichiro went streaking past and beat him to the base.

"Safe!" Ichiro had beaten out an infield hit!

The crowd roared its approval as Johnson stomped back to the mound. He and Helton had played the ball perfectly, yet Ichiro had still gotten a hit.

Now former Mariner Alex Rodriguez stepped into the batter's box. Some Mariners fans, still stinging over the fact that Rodriguez had left the team and signed with Texas, booed when he was introduced. Yet at the same time, they wanted him to get a hit and knock Ichiro in.

Most players hold back a little bit in the All-Star Game, not wanting to risk injury. Few try for diving catches or stolen bases. But Ichiro knew how to play the game only one way: with his best possible effort. He knew that Johnson took a long time winding up and that he could steal second if he got a good jump.

So far in the season, he had stolen 28 bases. Rodriguez had two strikes already. After taking a close look at Johnson's windup, Ichiro broke for second base.

He got a fabulous jump and beat the throw easily as Rodriguez struck out. A stolen base for Ichiro!

Unfortunately, the American League left him stranded. Ichiro played several more innings and came to bat twice more. Although he failed to get another hit, the American League, keyed by a Cal Ripken home run and the solid pitching of Freddy Garcia, won the game 4–1. Now Ichiro and his teammates looked forward to the remainder of the season.

In a little more than half a season in the major leagues, Ichiro had already made a bigger splash than many players make in their entire careers. As he prepared for the second half, he was determined to do even better. Although the Mariners had a huge lead in the AL West, they weren't taking anything for granted.

But just after the All-Star Game, Ichiro was troubled by several incidents. His All-Star Game appearance had sparked even more interest in him among the Japanese media. On one occasion, Ichiro reported that he was driving and was "nearly forced to stop his car" when he was blinded by flashbulbs from the cameras of Japanese press photographers. Another time, a Japanese newspaper managed to eavesdrop on a conversation that Ichiro was having on his cell phone, and the paper printed a story about Ichiro's private conversation. For the first time all season, off-the-field incidents would affect his game.

Ichiro struggled in the first two games after the break, collecting only one hit. After the second game, however, Ichiro and teammate Kazuhiro Sasaki, who was also tired of the press, announced that they were boycotting Japanese media — they refused to speak to any Japanese reporters.

The Japanese press was offended, primarily because most of Ichiro and Sasaki's problems stemmed from one gossip-heavy tabloid called *Friday*. Nevertheless, Ichiro and Sasaki were determined to protect their privacy at all costs.

While the controversy raged, Ichiro continued to slump, failing to get a hit in four consecutive games and dropping his average to .325, his lowest point since mid-April. Some people in baseball viewed the slump as proof that American pitchers were finally learning how to pitch to Ichiro. Others thought he was beginning to wear down in the season, which is more than thirty games longer than the Japanese season. But in reality, he was distracted by outside events.

Seattle officials tried to ease the situation by instituting new rules designed to help Ichiro deal with the press. The Mariners limited the media's contact with Ichiro to a brief press conference after each game. The press backed off a little, and Ichiro and Sasaki lifted their boycott.

As soon as that happened, Ichiro went on a long hot streak, collecting at least one hit in 34 of his next 35 games and lifting his batting average back up to .347. At the same time, the Mariners kept winning, solidifying their hold on the division lead.

Ichiro was more popular than ever before. When the Mariners held a promotion and gave away Ichiro bobblehead dolls before one game, fans showed up hours before the start to make sure they received a doll. A rap singer wrote a song about Ichiro and the Mariners played it over their stadium sound system. And Mariners fans in right field started calling that section of the stands "Area 51" in honor of Ichiro's number.

Entering August, the Mariners' record was a stellar 77–30, a pace that put them on course to win more games in one season than any team in baseball history. The 1906 Chicago Cubs held the all-time record of 116 games, but if the Mariners kept winning, a new record was in reach.

# Chapter Nine:
## 2001

### Record Performances

Ichiro grabbed his third Rookie of the Month Award in August as the Mariners maintained their winning ways. Ichiro batted an incredible .429 for the month to lift his average to .350. Seattle had locked up the division title, so for the rest of the season the Mariners and their fans turned their attention to the record books.

If the Mariners could keep winning in September and early October, they had a good shot at breaking the Cubs' record of 116 wins in one season. Only three years earlier, in 1998, the New York Yankees had set an American League record by winning 114 regular season games. When they followed that performance by winning the World Series, many people called them the greatest team of all time. Now, some were starting to say the same thing about the Mariners.

Seattle Mariners Bret Boone and Mike Cameron had been enjoying the best two seasons of their major league careers, but the biggest difference between the Mariners of 2000 and the Mariners of 2001 was Ichiro. He helped the team change from one that depended on the home run to one that was built around speed and defense. Ichiro was already considered a shoo-in for the American League Rookie of the Year Award, and many also considered him a top contender for the American League Most Valuable Player Award. No American League player had won both awards in the same season since Boston Red Sox outfielder Fred Lynn in 1975.

Mariners fans were going wild in the late season. By early September more than three million fans had poured into Safeco Field.

Ichiro and his teammates were determined to maintain focus in the final month and enter the playoffs with confidence. In one early September game versus the Baltimore Orioles, Ichiro demonstrated that he was playing just as hard now as he had played earlier in the season.

Ichiro led off the game with a first inning single to set the team record for most hits in a season at 215, putting him within reach of the league rookie record of 233 set by Joe Jackson in 1911. But Ichiro was just getting started.

Ichiro immediately stole second, went to third base on a long fly out, and then scored on a ground ball to give the Mariners the lead. Then, in the third inning, he led off with a home run. Two innings later, his glove and arm proved to be the difference.

With an Oriole runner on second base, Jerry Hairston singled to right field.

Ichiro was ready. He knew the Oriole base runner would probably try to score on a single, so he charged in hard and came up throwing.

The throw came toward home on a line, and Seattle catcher Dan Wilson blocked the plate as he caught the ball a split second before the runner came crashing home. He swiped him with a quick tag. Out!

The play took the steam out of the Orioles and the Mariners rolled to a 6–1 win, their 102nd of the season. After the game Mariner pitcher Joel Pineiro gave Ichiro full credit for the win, saying "He hits home runs, he throws guys out, whatever. He is amazing."

As the months progressed, speculation about the

playoffs and the World Series crowded the sports pages. Then something happened that pushed all other headlines into the background. On September 11, terrorists attacked the World Trade Center in New York City and the Pentagon in Washington, D.C. Like many other people all over the world, Ichiro was shocked and saddened by the events of September 11. Thousands of people of all nationalities, including several hundred Japanese, had been killed. The baseball season was suspended for a week to give everyone a chance to come to terms with the tragedy.

When baseball resumed on September 18, fans and players alike looked forward to the opportunity to put the tragedy aside for a few hours. Despite their feelings of sadness, Ichiro and the Mariners were still able to maintain their high level of play for the rest of the month. Ichiro earned his fourth Rookie of the Month Award for the season. Only a few games remained in the regular season, and the Mariners still had a chance to set the all-time record for wins. With Ichiro on the field, it seemed as if anything were possible.

The Mariners surpassed the Yankees' mark with

their 115th win on October 6 versus Texas, taking the game 6–2 as Ichiro chipped in with a single and scored a run. With two games left in the season, they could still beat the all-time record.

But the Mariners knew that if they set a record and then lost in the playoffs, the achievement would mean little. So in the last two games of the season manager Lou Piniella decided to give some of his key players, including Ichiro, some rest before the playoffs.

Despite the fact that Ichiro was sitting on the bench, the Mariners defeated Texas 1–0 for their 116th win to tie the all-time record. But in the final game of the season, they lost to the Rangers, 4–3, to finish with a record of 116–46.

Ichiro and his teammates were ready for the playoffs. Over the course of the season Ichiro had more than answered the questions surrounding his ability, finishing with a .350 batting average — the best in the American League — 127 runs scored, and 56 stolen bases. No one was saying that pitchers would figure him out or that he would tire at the end of the season anymore. He had proven that a Japanese position player could succeed in the major leagues. There was already speculation that his success would lead other talented Japanese stars to follow him to the United States.

Yet Ichiro knew that neither his batting average nor the Mariners' record meant anything in the playoffs. Every batter starts out with a .000 batting average and every team starts with the same 0–0 record in the playoffs. As he said after the last game of the regular season, "To me, what I have won is not important. To me what is important is how I prepare for the game every day." He was already looking ahead to the playoffs. Everyone on the team knew that if they didn't make it to the World Series and win the championship, the season would be a disappointment.

They faced the Central Division champion Cleveland Indians in the best-of-five division series. Although Seattle had defeated Cleveland in eight of twelve games during the regular season, the Mariners weren't taking the Indians lightly. With a potent hitting force keyed by slugger Jim Thome and Roberto Alomar, and a pitching staff built around the hard-throwing Bartolo Colon and rookie star C. C. Sabathia, the Indians promised to provide stiff competition.

The series opened in Seattle. Although the weather was perfect, the late afternoon sun cast a shadow across the diamond, making it difficult for hitters to see the ball.

Every hitter but Ichiro, that is. He pounded Indian pitcher Bartolo Colon for three hits. But Colon was able to keep the other Mariners in check and the Indians pecked away at pitcher Freddy Garcia to emerge with a 5–0 win.

"I was relieved," said Ichiro after the game in reference to his standout performance. But he was disappointed that they had lost the game. During the regular season, Ichiro had collected three hits in 26 different games, and the Mariners had won 23 of them.

Determined to turn it around in game two, the Mariners turned to veteran pitcher Jamie Moyer. In the bottom of the first inning, Seattle batters did their best to make Moyer's job easy.

Ichiro started things off by working Indian starter Chuck Finley for a walk to lead off the first inning.

Moments later, Mike Cameron hit a home run to put the Mariners ahead. They never looked back and rolled to a 5–1 win.

The two clubs traveled to Cleveland for game three. Although Ichiro singled to start the game and later scored to give Seattle a quick 1–0 lead, the Indians pounded a series of Seattle pitchers, romping to a 17–2 win. In order to advance to the American League Championship Series for the chance to win the pennant and reach the World Series, the Mariners would have to win the next two games. If they lost, their season was over.

There was some question about whether or not game four would even be played. It rained hard in Cleveland, causing the start of the game to be held up.

While they waited for the skies to clear, most Mariners were nervous. They paced back and forth or played cards in the clubhouse.

But Ichiro was calm. He had brought along his favorite pillow and stretched out in the clubhouse and took a nap.

Finally, the game started. Ichiro felt fresh and relaxed. Mariner Freddy Garcia and Cleveland ace Bartolo Colon both pitched well early in the game, holding down the batters of each team with ease. Entering the seventh inning, however, Seattle trailed 1–0. They were running out of time.

But Colon tired. In the seventh inning the Mariners loaded the bases and pushed across the tying run. Then, with runners on first and second and two outs, Ichiro came to bat.

There was no player manager Lou Piniella wanted at the plate more than Ichiro. During the regular season he had been one of Seattle's best clutch hitters, batting nearly .450 during the regular season with men in scoring position.

On the Cleveland bench, Indians manager Charlie Manuel tried to decide what to do. He could walk Ichiro and force the go-ahead run to third base, change pitchers, or have Colon pitch to the Japanese superstar. He hesitated a moment, then decided to leave Colon in the game. He then flashed a signal to his catcher to have Colon pitch to Ichiro.

Colon was precisely the kind of pitcher many had expected to give Ichiro trouble, a hard thrower who wasn't afraid to pitch inside. But Ichiro had been proving his critics wrong all year long.

He did so again. When one of Colon's pitches

floated out over the plate, Ichiro slashed at it and drove the ball into left field. Two runners scored and the Mariners led, 3–1. It was Ichiro's ninth hit of the series, giving him a playoff batting average of .563.

The Mariners hung on to win 6–2 and force the series to a fifth game. After the contest, one reporter asked Piniella if he had wanted Ichiro at the plate in the seventh inning with the game on the line.

The cagy manager just smiled and said, "You know he's going to make good contact. He's got 244 hits in the regular season. The answer is 'Yes.'"

The Indians expressed amazement at Ichiro's play. Batting coach Gerald Perry called him "a magician. What he can do with a bat in his hands is remarkable."

The two teams returned to Seattle for the finale. Jamie Moyer pitched for Seattle against Chuck Finley.

Once again, Ichiro was in the middle of the action. He cracked three more hits and scored an insurance run in the seventh inning of the Mariners' 3–1 win. Seattle would advance to the American League Championship Series and play the defending champion New York Yankees for the pennant!

Ichiro had been magnificent. In five games he had

gone 12-for-20 for a .600 batting average. As one reporter commented afterward, "There is no MVP awarded in the Division Series, but if there was, the Japanese right fielder should get it."

But Ichiro didn't care about that. He just wanted to keep on playing until he had helped make the Mariners world champions.

# Chapter Ten:
## 2001

## Season's End

Although Seattle's regular season record was far better than New York's, the Yankees were world champions and the Mariners knew they wouldn't go down without fighting. They were a talented, experienced team that after the tragedy of September 11 had come to symbolize the spirit of New York City. Many baseball fans who otherwise would have been pulling for the Mariners found themselves rooting for New York.

Both teams entered the league series confident of victory. One sportswriter called the series a matchup of "the best team in baseball against the best team in baseball," because although the Mariners had the best record in 2001, the Yankees were the defending champions and a legendary team.

The Yankees knew that in order to stop the Mariners, they would have to stop Ichiro. The Mariners knew that in order to beat the Yankees, they needed Ichiro to get on base.

Game one perfectly illustrated the latter fact. The series opened in Seattle and New York starter Andy Pettitte kept Ichiro off base early. The Yankees, meanwhile, jumped out to an early 3–0 lead. Ichiro didn't reach base until the ninth inning, when he doubled and scored a run. But by then it was too late. The Mariners lost, 4–2.

"Keeping Ichiro off base made pitching to the rest of the lineup less stressful," said Yankees manager Joe Torre.

Game two was critical for the Mariners. They knew they couldn't afford to fall two games behind in the series.

Ichiro got the Mariners off to a good start when he singled to open the game. Unfortunately, his teammates failed to bring him home. Then, in the third inning, he drove the ball deep into the outfield and reached base on an error. But once again his teammates failed to knock him home.

Meanwhile, the Yankees scored three early runs

and hung on for a 3–2 win. Ichiro and the Mariners were in tough shape.

The series moved to New York. At first it looked as if the Mariners would go down to a quick defeat in game three as the Yankees jumped ahead 2–0. But in the middle of the game the Mariners exploded. Bret Boone knocked in five runs and Ichiro scored twice on a hit and two walks. Seattle won in a rout, 14–3.

But the victory would be the 120th and last of the season for the Mariners. In the next two games Ichiro was held to only one hit, and New York won 3–1 and 12–3 to win the pennant and advance to the World Series.

Manager Lou Piniella was philosophical after the last game. "I'm proud of what our organization has accomplished this year and I'm proud of my players," he said. And of all the players on the Mariners, there was no player he was more proud of than Ichiro.

In one year Ichiro had gone from being a virtual unknown rookie to being hailed as one of the best players in the game. He had won the American League batting title and led his team to a record-setting season. He had overcome every challenge and had proven that not only could Japanese position players make the grade in Major League Baseball, but they could become stars. He had fulfilled his lifelong dream.

Ichiro was still disappointed to have lost the pennant race. While the Arizona Diamondbacks played the Yankees in the World Series, eventually defeating the Yankees in seven games, Ichiro tried to stay out of the spotlight. After a few days of rest, he began working out in preparation for the 2002 season. He was determined to improve.

But he didn't stay out of the spotlight for long. In the weeks following the end of the baseball season, major league officials reveal which players have won individual awards for the season. Over the next month, Ichiro accumulated honor after honor.

He first learned that he had been named to the "Silver Slugger" team of the best hitters in the game, as selected by the managers and coaches. Next he discovered that he had also won a Gold Glove Award as one of the best three defensive outfielders in the American League.

Ichiro was particularly proud of the Gold Glove.

When he first came to the major leagues, he was determined to prove that he was a complete player, and the award provided evidence that he was. "I appreciate that I was chosen for this award," he said, "because it's not usually my defense that gets recognized. My goal is to play solid defense rather than putting an emphasis on flashy play."

A few days later, Ichiro collected another award. He was named American League Rookie of the Year, collecting 27 of a possible 28 first-place votes from the Baseball Writers Association of America. Although he was pleased, he explained, "Looking back at what I had done in Japan, I was a little embarrassed to be called a rookie in the United States. But I had never played here and was a rookie with the Mariners."

He then thanked the Seattle fans for their support. "The fans and many people in the Mariners organization made it easy for me to relax and have good preparation," he said.

Major League Baseball saves the biggest award, the Most Valuable Player Award, for last. Ichiro was expected to contend for the award, but most people believed it would be given to Jason Giambi of the

Oakland Athletics, who had also won the award in 2000. Others thought it might go to Ichiro's teammate, Bret Boone, who had led the league with 141 RBIs.

Ichiro didn't really expect to win. No one had ever won the batting title, Rookie of the Year, and MVP in the same season, and both Boone and Giambi were deserving.

But on November 20, Ichiro was thrilled to learn that he had been selected as the Most Valuable Player in the American League. Although he had won the award three times in Japan, "they cannot be compared," he said. He considered his selection as American League MVP much more significant than his earlier awards in Japan.

It was a close ballot, as Ichiro won by only eight votes over Jason Giambi, with teammate Bret Boone a close third. Ichiro let everyone know that he would not allow the award to go to his head or make him change his approach. Although he hoped to improve in 2002, he told reporters not to expect him to try to hit home runs.

"If I try to hit for more power, I will lose what I do as a baseball player," he said. For Ichiro, that mattered more than anything else. Individual accomplishments were nice, but performing to the best of his ability and doing everything possible to help his team win were more important to Ichiro. He told the press how much he appreciated the talents of his teammate Boone, and how much he looked forward to playing with Boone in the future to help the Mariners achieve their ultimate goal of a world championship.

"I hope," said Ichiro of Boone, "that we can eat from the same rice bowl again next season."

# Chapter Eleven:
## 2002–2003

### Rookie No More

Ichiro had more than proven himself his rookie year. But he knew that he had to perform just as well in 2002. Otherwise, his 2001 performance was sure to be considered a fluke. When he reported to spring training, he was looking forward to making the most of the upcoming season.

"More than getting better or improving every day, it's more of being able to show your best performance every day," he said in one interview. "That's what I strive for."

"Last year is gone," he added. "It's history. I just want to build on my experiences from last year and hopefully have another great season."

In some ways, Ichiro's sophomore year was a bit easier than his rookie season. The media frenzy that had surrounded him the previous year had died down to a dull roar, allowing him to concentrate more fully on the game at hand. He also had a better idea of what to expect on the field. He was no longer the new kid, but a seasoned player who had adjusted to the major leagues.

Of course, the opposition had also had time to adjust to Ichiro, too. In the off season, they studied film of the Japanese player's many hitting styles. Watching him steal bases and chase down fly balls brought home just how fast he really was. When they entered the 2002 season, they had learned not to underestimate him.

None of that seemed to matter. In the first two months, he knocked the ball around the field, going 17 for 45 during an 11-game hitting streak in early April, then adding a second, 12-game streak in early May and a third, 15-game streak starting in late May. The last two times, his batting average approached the .500 mark, helping raise his overall average to .404 by the end of May, the best in the league. His performance left many baseball watchers wondering if perhaps he might be the first player since Red Sox slugger Ted Williams in 1952 to end the season with an average of more than .400.

It was in a game against the Red Sox on May 10 that Ichiro showed just how good a player he was. In the first inning, he got on base due to a throwing error by shortstop Nomar Garciaparra. He reached second when his teammate Mark McLemore singled. Then he stole third, putting him in position to score — which he did when Bret Boone singled.

In the second inning, Ichiro motored to first on an infield single to Sox pitcher Frank Castillo. He had a safe trip around the rest of the bases when McLemore homered.

Ichiro led off the fifth inning with a walk. Then he stole second. And third. And when Ruben Sierra knocked a single to second, he scored his third run to bring the Mariners score to five.

By the seventh inning, Seattle was leading Boston 6–2 — a good lead, but one that Boston could still overcome in the remaining innings. Jeff Cirillo grounded out to second, bringing Ichiro up to bat. So far, Ichiro had made it to first base on an error, a walk, and a single. This time, however, he slugged the ball to deep right field. By the time the dust settled, he was standing on third. Once again, he scored when McLemore singled. The Mariners took the game, 7–2.

"Ichiro's a great player," Red Sox manager Grady Little commented after the game. "He's a tough cookie and with that kind of speed he puts pressure on a defense."

By the All-Star break in July, Ichiro was leading the American League with an average of .358. It seemed that the small player from Japan had hit his stride.

But in August, that stride suddenly broke. After logging some solid games in July, including his first multi-homer outing on July 13, Ichiro went into a slump that he just couldn't seem to snap out of. The Mariners, too, went into a nosedive, moving from first place to third behind the A's and the Angels. There would be no World Series run for them.

Ichiro ended the season with a batting average of .321, 208 hits, 111 runs scored, and 31 steals. Had 2002 been his first year in the major leagues, many would have considered these stats to be impressive. Unfortunately, however, the numbers were all less than those he'd earned the previous year, leading many critics to speculate that Ichiro didn't have what it took to stay on top.

Such criticism seemed to gain weight in 2003. Ichiro's performance was a near-duplicate of the previous year. After a slow start in early April, he picked up speed in May, June, and July. On July 18, he belted his first Major League grand-slam homer. But less than one week later, he went 0 for 6 for the first time in his Major League career.

After that, he seemed to tire. At season's end, his average was down from .321 in 2002 to .312, and although his hitting figure increased by 4 to 212, he had also been at bat 23 more times in 2003. Still, he led the League with multi-hit games (66) and was second in the AL in hits, fifth in stolen bases, seventh in batting average, and eighth in runs. For the third season in a row, he'd surpassed the 200-hit mark, making him the second player in League history to do so in his first three seasons. He also earned his third consecutive Gold Glove Award.

At the close of the 2003 season, Ichiro became eligible for salary arbitration, meaning that his next season's salary would be determined by an outside panel unless he and the Mariners came to a contract agreement. Despite Ichiro's lower stats, the Mariner management still believed wholeheartedly in their Japanese player — and they proved it in mid-December of 2003, when they offered him a four-year, $44-million contract to stay with the team. Ichiro agreed to the terms, ensuring that he would be a Mariner through 2007.

How will the Japanese superstar perform in the next four years? By all accounts, the outlook is good. If he continues to hit as well as he did in his first three seasons, he could become the first player in MLB history to reach four consecutive seasons with 200 or more hits. His speed on the base paths is undiminished, and with his rocket arm, he remains one of the best right fielders in the game.

To put it simply, to baseball fans worldwide, Ichiro is "ichiban" — number one.

**The #1 Sports Series for Kids**

# Read them all!

*Originally published as *Crackerjack Halfback*

Look Who's Playing First Base

Miracle at the Plate

Mountain Bike Mania

No Arm in Left Field

Nothin' but Net

Olympic Dream

Penalty Shot

Pressure Play

Prime-Time Pitcher

Red-Hot Hightops

The Reluctant Pitcher

Return of the Home Run Kid

Roller Hockey Radicals

Run, Billy, Run

Run for It

Shoot for the Hoop

Shortstop from Tokyo

Skateboard Renegade

Skateboard Tough

Slam Dunk

Snowboard Maverick

Snowboard Showdown

Soccer Duel

Soccer Halfback

Soccer Scoop

Spike It!

Stealing Home

The Submarine Pitch

Supercharged Infield

The Team That Couldn't Lose

Tennis Ace

Tight End

Too Hot to Handle

Top Wing

Touchdown for Tommy

Tough to Tackle

Wheel Wizards

Windmill Windup

Wingman on Ice

The Year Mom Won the Pennant

All available in paperback from Little, Brown and Company

# Matt Christopher®

## Sports Bio Bookshelf

Lance Armstrong

Kobe Bryant

Jennifer Capriati

Terrell Davis

Julie Foudy

Jeff Gordon

Wayne Gretzky

Ken Griffey Jr.

Mia Hamm

Tony Hawk

Grant Hill

Ichiro

Derek Jeter

Randy Johnson

Michael Jordan

Mario Lemieux

Tara Lipinski

Mark McGwire

Greg Maddux

Hakeem Olajuwon

Shaquille O'Neal

Alex Rodriguez

Curt Schilling

Briana Scurry

Sammy Sosa

Venus and
Serena Williams

Tiger Woods

Steve Young

CPSIA information can be obtained at www.ICGtesting.com
Printed in the USA
LVOW08s1930290713

345164LV00001B/42/P